*To i r...* (handwritten)

# ANDRE

*with* Chan'tel Grayson

*Thanks* (handwritten)

*From: Andrea* (handwritten)

# FOR SUCH A
# TIME AS THIS

*A Concise Memoir*

*I love you!* (handwritten)

# FOR SUCH A TIME AS THIS

---

*A Concise Memoir*

## ANDREA GRAYSON

*with* Chan'tel Grayson

ISBN-10: 1532949480
ISBN-13: 978-1532949487

# Dedication

To My Lord and Savior, Jesus Christ, who is the true Author and Finisher of my faith, and this book. For without His Word, my words would not have been.

*In the beginning was the Word, and the Word was with God, and the Word was God.*
*— John 1:1 (ESV)*

# Acknowledgements

Many years ago when I began writing, I knew that in order to completely heal my story had to be told. By the grace of God, the gifts necessary to do it were right here within me and my very own family.

I would like to thank all of *my people* who bore with me in love throughout the years to make this book possible, and encouraged me during this time of writing.

This is the fruit of all of our labor.

# Preface

My People,

I was the one who helped drive the nails further in the hands of Jesus Christ during His time of crucifixion. I was also the one who placed the crown of thorns upon His head and later gambled for His garments. He was the one who knew all that I had done, yet still chose to die for me. So, today, I choose to write for Him.

My writings reach high and low places.
My writings reach lit and dark places.
My writings open eyes to see and hearts to love.
My writings are anointed and full of purpose.
My writings hug, hold, and set captives free.

My writings are more about my healing than they are about my hurts.
My writings say I have suffered, but more importantly, they say that I am better because of it.


My writings tell a story that a little girl (me), along with many others, needs to hear.
My writings are the truth about me, **for you.**

The more of me…
I give to He…
The more of He…
Replaces me.

This is my prayer.

In Jesus name,
*Andrea Grayson*

# Contents

# Part I:
## The Little Girl

*Before I formed you in the womb I knew you, and*
*before you were born I set you apart....*
*— Jeremiah 1:5 (NIV)*

## *Once Upon a Time*

On November 19, 1963, a baby girl was born to a couple living in Oklahoma City, Oklahoma. Three days after she was born, one of the most famous and loved presidents in history, John F. Kennedy, was killed in Downtown, Dallas, Texas. Immediately after hearing this report, the world stood still. His death had put a damper on her birth, and as she cried to be noticed, her voice went unheard. At the time of birth, she had an unknown medical condition and growth within her mouth that the doctors deemed terminal. She was only expected to live through her pain until the age of 12. The sound of her high-pitched and squeaky cry was excruciating to the ears surrounding her. Being hushed up while in agony, the seed of rejection and emotional abandonment was planted. That seed plagued her as early as birth, and throughout the 40+ years of her life roaming through wilderness. Everything that happened thereafter, watered it.

The early memory that manifested in her mind was that of living in a two-bedroom house with four other siblings in the very Southeast corner of Idabel, Oklahoma.  It was only nine miles out of the city limits; this was called "the country". While her father continued his work in Oklahoma City, he eventually relocated the family to Idabel. He commuted back and forth from Idabel to Oklahoma City for work. Years later, she would learn that her half-sister was conceived during this time. In her mind, she belonged to the perfect family, especially after her father moved from the city to the country to be with them permanently. Her father enjoyed having kids and got a kick out of finding out that Mother was pregnant again. He was finally ready to be a father and a godly man. He wanted to create a solid foundation for the family to build upon and grow.

She perceived that they were all perfect for each other as a family. Dad and Mother were so young, yet did so much together in the home, the church, and the community. They would have family outings, picnics, cookouts, and go camping together. They would even allow her and her siblings to invite their classmates over and enjoy the privilege of being in the midst of a real family. Her parents would take all of them to church and they learned to know and acknowledge the love of Christ. They were taught to respect their elders and be grateful for the little things in life. Her dad was well-respected and highly favored. It seemed that everything he touched prospered, *big time!* One year, Dad won an award naming him the "man of the year in McCurtain county" for land renovation and conservation. She was so proud of him. Dad would often be so hurt when neighbors and relatives would steal his materials and animals. Yet and still, he modeled Christ, showing mercy toward them and offering them work in place of filing criminal charges. Daddy was home, and she looked upon him as her savior. He was now there to save her from this mean old world and the memories that had become embedded into her mind.

✝

At a very young preschool age, she was sexually molested by a trusted member in the community. As he sat in his car, his arm hung out of the car window, and he beckoned her to come closer with his hand. He acted innocently and lured her with endearing compliments and a manipulative tone. He would give empty promises not to hurt her, while whispering, "Relax, baby" as he dug his cold, black, and wrinkled fingers around inside of her. One of his hands was in her, while his other hand masturbated and fondled his genitals. It seemed like no one existed in the world in that moment except those two. Aside from the physical pain, the look of pleasure on his face told her that this was wrong and she couldn't tell a soul. She was sore for days thereafter, and bath time would give off a burning sensation. This was the first secret she ever kept.

It's ironic how the same house can feel different to siblings under the same roof. The excitement of belonging to a whole family had quickly diminished and her excitement for life did as well. This opened the door for demonic spirits that entangled the depth of her being. She knew that what had happened to her was not the normal child's play that she was accustomed to. The inner being of this little girl became enraged and fearful. She became afraid of life and her boundaries were non-existent. She didn't tell a soul or dare to mess up the image of the picture perfect family. This was the country way.

With a new infant sibling to care for, her mother had little attention to offer her. As the school year approached, more than anything, she did not want to be the only kid left home while her other school-aged siblings attended school. One of her brothers, who was only 14 months older would soon begin attending The Head Start Program. Although she was too young to attend, she cried hysterically to go with him, and her parents and the school overlooked her age and allowed her to attend; one year with him, and one year on her own.

As she learned to read, she began escaping through books; books that started with "Once upon at a time…", and ended in "Happily ever after". She became every character in these books and quickly began living in a utopia to escape her reality. It was real to her. If the character laid in the sun on the beach, so did she. If the character was swept off her feet, so was she. She sought out every book in this way. From then on, she became a performer. Like in the books, she was always interested in playing a role, but she was still seeking more. She turned to music and dancing and found that it soothed the savaged beast within her soul. She learned to move her body well to it and ceased many opportunities to do so. She wasn't exactly sure if the soothing was positive or negative, but the attention she received felt good.

She rarely played with classmates and didn't have many friends. Even on a playground surrounded by various children, she felt alone. This made her look down most of the time instead of looking into the eyes of her soul and learning who she was becoming.

By the time she was nine years old, books had become her best friends and she could hardly stand moments apart from them. They became a part of her every day existence. As time went on, she became a phenomenal reader, and had graduated to Nancy Drew and Hardy Boys mystery books, along with various romance novels. Yet still, she felt as if she was wearing a sign that read "Look at me, I'm hurting".

✝

With so many feelings of insecurity, betrayal, abandonment and nowhere in particular to place them, except within the shadows of her mind and the gutter of her very being, a self-destructive surface began to form.

She so greatly desired to be approved and accepted, that she began stealing for her grandmother (or "Momma" as the family called her), receiving praise as her payment. It pleased her to please *her*, and as she continued on, her bad habit grew rapidly. Her small pockets that held small amounts of stolen tobacco and snuff, were suddenly exchanged for large bags and purses to hold stolen items for her own enjoyment. The adrenaline rush she got from planning, pulling it off, not getting caught, and the expectation of the next time were reasons that propelled her mission. The more she stole, the greater she felt. It was invigorating. But, that feeling of invigoration was temporary, and only lasted until the moment she'd steal again. Euphoria had been a far-fetched feeling for so long. She'd gained a sense of entitlement, and so everything that she took, she took unapologetically, and she accepted the label of "kleptomaniac" by the many in her hometown.

The many things she stole, represented the many things that had been stolen from her. All the while, her innocence could never be restored again.

Momma only lived across the street. There were peddlers who would travel down the road selling fruits, vegetables, and or other goods in the country. And for Momma's sake, the little girl would pursue every male peddler that came around, in hopes of winning her approval. Because Momma's acceptance was only financially-driven, her approval didn't come cheap. The cost involved a back-room performance with random peddlers for money. The back room was always dark, damp, and eerie. The sound of zippers zipping up and down and the feeling of pats on the back for a job well done, made the little girl cringe. Ever since that day, it was if the satisfied hands who pat her back like a dog, left a residue that was difficult to scrub off. That moment on, until she would heal, hugs that included pats on her back, despite well intentions, would ignite feelings of anger and disgust.

At the end of a performance, Momma would intimidate the little girl and order her to "Go back across that street and don't tell anything that goes on in my house!". Momma didn't like the little girl's dad very much, and she knew that if he found out, he would surely rescue the little girl and put an end to her profitable business. I guess since Momma grew up on a plantation in Louisiana, where the women were the Master's mates, she saw nothing wrong with selling her own seed. And so she did, about twice a week. When Momma would stop by and say "Come on, you're coming with me!" the little girl knew what was next. She would return home again muted with shame, as fear silenced her voice.

As life went on, the void in heart became deeper, the whole became darker, and her countenance became sadder. She had lost herself and felt as if all of her experiences were out of body. She felt sorry for that little girl. Every wrong thing that the little girl did was easily justified by her pain. The only hope for acceptance truly came from her savior, which was her father. He always knew just the right words to say and make her feel loved. When she desired to go out, he would make sure to express that his little girl would be missed. Hope came from him, and also later from her 2nd grade school teacher, who seemed to see more in her than she did in herself.

At the end of her 2nd grade school year, she received for a third year in a row, a perfect attendance award. She had also now become a teacher's aide. Performance remained important, and yet another performance had gone well, and granted her a seat right up front next to Ms. Smith.

Finally, all of that reading was beginning to pay off. Her 2nd grade school teacher submitted paperwork to the Board of Education on her behalf. The two of them went to Oklahoma City and there she took several state tests and was eventually promoted to the 3rd grade. This opened the doors for jealousy, envy, and hate amongst her classmates. There were times when her teacher would place her hand under the little girl's chin and tell her to look within her eyes. She appreciated Ms. Smith. Ms. Smith saw something in her, and in a way, Ms. Smith was rescuing her from something that little girl just couldn't discuss.

One particular school day during her 4th grade year, her Principal had a heart attack, which resulted in school closure for the day. All students were ordered to leave school grounds and take a bus to a neighboring school located about 8 miles uptown. Little did she know, this trip would be enlightening and give her a positive sense of identity.

Being called "Andre" by everyone for all of her life, she had no idea how to respond to this teacher who called her "Andrea" during roll call. The teacher called the foreign name multiple times before gaining a response. "Andrea?", "Andrea?", "Andrea Grayson?" She had never heard her name pronounced like that, and honestly, only knew to finally respond when it was followed by her last name. This was a monumental moment, and the little girl could not *wait* to get on the bus after school and announce to everyone that her name was not Andre. She was eager to announce to all, that she was *not* the girl that they had thought she was. She was excited to proclaim that she was new! She had become another person within the same day of going to another school and was so glad about it.

While her grades excelled, she would rather cheat to get a dishonest A, then to settle for receiving an honest B. It was still all about performance. The feeling of dumbness was not worth it to her. Notes here and there written on her hand reminding here that "I" came before "E" except after "C" were deemed absolutely necessary.

†

Her search for the right perspective and the proper placement of all of these unhealthy emotions resulted in extra anxiety and disillusions. With her mind always racing and her hands always busy, she found a comforting distraction in meeting the needs of others, while

simultaneously neglecting her own. The hurt
was helping the hurt, and although it
temporarily filled voids within her, it became all
the more dysfunctional and destructive than her
former coping mechanisms. The demons inside
of her perverted her coddling ways and made
her mentally ill. She performed in various ways
to obtain love, and this "care" that she gave
became a seemingly promising way of escaping
her reality. Although her physical body was tired
of the self-afflicted abuse, mentally, it was the
only solution she could formulate in her mind,
and it took a great toll. She sympathized for the
suffering little girl. This little girl was trapped in
an imaginary life. She never seemed to be good
enough, yet continuously strived for perfection
in hopes of unlocking an unknown truth, that
she had been good enough all along.

†

Dad had gotten sick. He was suddenly
diagnosed with cancer, and was given only a
short time to live. That summer the little girl
and her Mother stayed in the hospital with Dad
as much as possible. During this time, her eldest
sister was enlisted to care for everyone and
everything pertaining to the house and her
siblings.

The little girl thought surely her dad would
regain his weight and get out of that bed. She

11

was full of hope and couldn't face the fact that he was potentially dying. She just *had* to be there as often as she could to witness the miracle. At times, she would often overhear Mother negotiating with the on-duty nurses to allow the little girl to stay with him, and supervise her while she ran errands.

The summer whipped by and her 7th grade school year was beginning. Sadly, the little girl's hospital visits came to an abrupt, mandatory end. She didn't want to go to school, but she had to, and it crushed her.

Only the second week into the 7th grade, she and her siblings were suddenly called into the school office. Their hearts were aware of the news before their ears were; their father, her savior, had died. Her oldest brother drove them all home from school that day, and it seemed like the longest drive home ever.

The Doctors were right. Cancer had eaten Dad quickly, and he died the 90th day, just as they had predicted. Her summer had been spent literally watching death take a toll upon her savior, only two months before her twelfth birthday. Though the doctors were correct about dad, they were incorrect about the little girl. Despite the growth that remained in her mouth over the years, she was "beating the odds", as Mother would say angrily. Maybe

Mother was upset with the doctors for misinforming her about her daughter and being accurate about her husband. Whatever the reason was, the little girl's existence had never been celebrated. With a pronounced death sentence of 12 years, maybe Mother figured there was no cause for celebration.

## *Changes in the House*

The house wasn't the same anymore and there was little support from family across the street, if that's what you want to call them. Rumors of jealousy filled the air, and at the worst time possible, all of the rumors appeared to be true.

Following her dad's death, the little girl and her 6 siblings began piling up and sleeping together in the same room with Mother. There was no conductor that orchestrated this arrangement, it just sort of happened. Without a word to one another about their pain, their individualistic patterns that were present in daylight were collective at nighttime.

She was numb to the core and began rebelling against everything she was raised to believe. She started clowning around and misbehaving in order to get attention, but of course, all the attention she received was negative and never satisfied her craving for true love and affection.

She stopped believing what her dad had taught her. She was angry, full of shame, and had countless doubts of the truth. Rebellion had become her official way out of the hell that she was living in and even at this young age, in her eyes, there was no more God. She was so upset with Dad for dying and leaving her and so upset with God for taking him. How could the God of her father allow this to happen to her? How could she believe that God was who He said He was, and all of this was working together for her good? She wanted no parts of Him and sought to get even with Him and show Him how she felt; she was becoming a god of her own world.

Dad was a noble deacon in the local church and his strict hands upon her life had made a huge impact. But there was no more structure, and discipline had died with him. She no longer had to worry about getting in trouble by him. She no longer had to worry about seeking his approval or disappointing him. Dad was gone, and unless he returned, there would be no remorse or consequences for her negative actions.

Mother wasn't at all a disciplinarian, and because of her great guilt, shame, and grief, she allowed the little girl and her siblings to do just about anything they wanted; she was lenient. Things had gone array and they all ran amok. Mother didn't make them go to school, she didn't make them abide by a curfew, and she didn't even make them call her mother. She wanted to be their friend, she wanted them to know that they were loved by her, and enabling them was her way of doing so.

✝

Mother was depressed, and in less than a year of Dad's death, she had entered into a new relationship with a man who seemed to have appeared out of nowhere, and it wasn't long before Mother had allowed him to move in and invade their space. I guess he was the rebound and it was Mother's way of handling her own grief and nostalgia for companionship. Dad died in September 1975, and her youngest half-brother, was born in October 1976. He was like her child, really, and many thought he was too. Mother's depression had extracted so much of her strength that she couldn't care for him on her own. The little girl's little brother was her little baby. And while her brother was a blessing to her, his dad, however, seemed like a curse.

Mother's grief was at its peak during this time, so much, that it affected her boyfriend. His pain triggered that of the little girl's and ignited an inappropriate, yet overwhelming sense of compassion within her. The little girl pitied him and he knew it, and he began making it a habit of quietly tip-toeing into the little girl's room late *every* night for the fulfillment of his sexual fantasies. There she was again, being there for everybody else, yet no one was there for her.

Of the numerous times the little girl tried to tell Mother about his sexual abuse, her mother simply could not bear hearing the truth. The little girl's fears tormented her and caused her to shake often, have trouble sleeping, and pee in the bed. She was losing weight and had horrible chest pains. Combined with her repeat acts of trouble-making, she became familiar with frequent visits to mental institutions with Mother, which involved countless interviews and examinations. Even then, the attention was nice. However, she found it oddly comical that the more she told to the doctors, the more diagnoses they would come up with. She was diagnosed with Borderline Personality Disorder. It was like a game. There was a name for everything *she* said, and a pill for everything *they* said.

Despite all of the abuse that little girl was experiencing, she still felt sorry for her mother. She couldn't understand why her mother would allow a man like this into their home. Surely she thought, Mother was being threatened, but later she discovered that Mother was only afraid. The little girl sympathized again, as she knew all too well the stifling ways of fear.

It was always something. It seemed to be one perverted encounter after another, and before she ever had the opportunity to heal from the last, she was suffering the trauma all over again, developing a repertoire of wounds.

†

Mother's boyfriend lived with them for a couple of years and his presence stirred up a lot of tension and animosity. He was so jealous of anyone who showed interest in the little girl, and even her classmates perceived him to be a sick man. He molested the little girl every…single…night.

His stay was overextended in the eyes of all the children, and he lived in the house with them up until the time her favorite uncle pulled a gun on him and nearly shot him in the head. Her uncle had attempted to shoot him on several occasions, but every time her uncle pointed the shotgun at him, he would hurl the little girl in front of the barrel of the gun to avoid getting shot, even while her little brother, his own son, remained on the little girl's hip.

Her uncle knew something was going on. During his frequent visits to the house, he would inquire repeatedly about what was wrong with her. "You keeping a secret?", he would ask, as he peered into her face, gazing intently into her eyes. He said she wasn't the same little happy girl that he was used to meddling. He said she had changed and was sad and quiet now. He knew something wasn't right, and he was right about it, but the little girl was helpless and could do nothing about it.

One night, her uncle took it upon himself to install a lock on the little girl's door to protect her from unwanted entries. He knew who that was. He stayed the night and slept on the floor in her room with his head facing the door. Sure enough, in the middle of the night, he heard her abuser approach the door with his butter knife trying to pry his way in. Immediately, her uncle turned to her and said, "That will be the last time he'll ever get a chance to put his hands on you."

After the final shotgun attempt, Mother's boyfriend moved out, but that didn't stop his attacks. He began kidnapping her little brother; her baby. He knew just what to do to agonize her and inflict more pain. Finally, one of her older brothers fought him, and that put an end to his shenanigans. The last they all had heard of him after that was he had a massive heart attack and died.

## School Clothes

One day, Mother received a phone call. Upon ending the call, Mother had informed the little girl that she would be sending her a few hours up North, just outside of "the country", to babysit her younger cousins for the summer. Her older cousin and her cousin's husband would be expecting her, and the little girl didn't have a choice. She wasn't asked her thoughts; she was just told how it all would work. What happened this summer could not compare to the former, but it certainly was not better in the slightest.

Money was scarce and the only way Mother could afford the little girl's school clothes for the upcoming year, would be in exchange for "babysitting" services. Initially, the little girl felt excited and a bit nervous, but the thought of being sent away did bring on an entirely different bout of loneliness. She felt as if she was being exiled from the safest place there was, which actually wasn't safe at all. Little did she know, during this summer break, she would be sexually abused in every way possible by her older cousin's husband, the father of the home.

Her cousin and her husband had 4 boys, not much younger than the little girl, and who were perfectly capable of watching themselves. What kind of arrangement was this? The little girl would quickly learn the truth; the school clothes were costly, and she was definitely not there to babysit, and needed a babysitter of her own.

Her cousins lived in a 2-story house, and while her cousin was at work, her cousin's husband would lock his boys in the upstairs room and escort the little girl to the family den. There he would perform daily, every sexual act imaginable upon her body until she became all too familiar with the feeling of being sexually abused.

He had put so much fear into her life and made sure to control his home with an ironclad set of rules that imparted hate into the hearts of everyone there. He did a great job of preserving his big and bad image. In front of all of them, he would grab cats and other animals and tear them apart with his bare hands to make sure that they all knew how strong he was, and how much control he had in his home. He would fling the head of the cat in one direction, and its body in the other, laugh, and go about his business.

Several times that summer, at least twice a month, the little girl would have panic attacks and her older cousin would take her to the emergency room. There she would undergo electrocardiograms (EKGs) amongst other tests, and be prescribed irrelevant antacid liquid medications which never cured any of her symptoms. The old habit of peeing in the bed had also re-surfaced, and the embarrassing habit would remain until adulthood.

It took a while before she was aware that her older cousin and the boys knew of the sexual abuse and the horrible things taking place within their home. They all knew that this man was ill-minded and perverse, but it was not their kingdom to rule and they had no authority to speak in it. The boys shared that they had heard the sounds of torment and abuse coming from the den, and one day, during the little girl's explanation to the boys of what their father had been doing to her, the little girl began performing every act on the eldest, just the way that she had been taught in her Summer course of sexual abuse. The abused had now become the abuser, and while she would later receive the forgiveness of the eldest son, the truth would remain that she had taken his virginity, never to be returned again. As little as the little girl was, she had never gotten the opportunity to be just that…a little girl.

Upon starting the next school term, thanks to her older cousin's husband, her body had developed at an accelerated rate and it looked like that of a woman. She often felt ashamed and embarrassed by the many comments made to her about the shape of her body and frame. Big, baggy clothes became her wardrobe of preference; anything to hide her curves and ward off potential suitors.

Once she was a bit older, she told Mother about her horrible "babysitting" experience. Mother's response was mute, but she believed that Mother had known all along what the arrangement entailed.

The thought of the possibility of Mother actually knowing what her little girl had encountered to receive school clothes hurt her, and sadly, it had non-verbally communicated that the little girl's body was not valuable, and prostitution was okay. In that moment, yet another demonic seed was being planted within her.

✝

Her high school years remained performance-based, and she continued to pour herself into books. She was never involved in sports, but she was a member of the student council and upward bound, and her scholastic achievements landed her on the principal's honor roll every semester and eventually in the Who's Who Among American High School Students.

She had fulfilled majority of her credits and by the time she reached the 10th and 11th grade, she had 3 free hours to be accounted for. There was a teacher who requested her assistance, and for the next two school years, she would be her Aide in a Special Education classroom. She was encouraged by the teacher to tutor a particular male student, and overtime, he began expressing interest in her by bringing her money, gifts, and becoming jealous of her interactions with other male peers.

She lacked camaraderie amongst her female peers, so majority of the peers she hung out with were males. Her female peers had ulterior motives, and only occasionally pursued "friendships" with her in hopes of attracting the attention of one of her brothers. They also made it a habit to attract the attention of any guys that she expressed interest in and proceeded to steal them from her. They would offer them more than she was willing to. It was like a hurtful competition that she didn't sign up for, that always resulted in rejection. They expressed jealousy regarding her body's physical development, while the males held her in high regard during a time where her self-esteem was low as ever. The few real friends that she had were outcasts. They were the ones that no one else wanted to claim as their own.

The pains of rejection had turned to ingrained bitterness and manifested in the form of self-destructive behaviors. There seemed to be no escape from her reality. Everywhere she went, there she was. She just couldn't get away from the pain of this little girl! She started smoking marijuana, and it did exactly what she wanted it to do, and more. It allowed her to forget, to giggle, and it increased her appetite. It also brought on depression and paranoia that in time she'd see would take a great toll on her. As life became more challenging, it would only be a temporary fix. One thing would lead to another as she searched for a greater fix to the issues of her life.

A United States Air Force recruiter came to her high school on the hunt for those with high grade point averages, and she was the sole qualifying candidate in search of an escape. She knew very little about what she was signing up for, and being only 17, Mother had to give parental consent for her to enlist. She had always wanted to help others, and did so to the best of her ability.

She would often see starving children with flies surrounding them on television and be moved with compassion. She thought that maybe the Air Force would somehow allow her the opportunity to go, feed and clothe the poor, hungry and destitute in a Third World Country of some sort. That passion burned within her and she looked forward to the opportunities that awaited her.

The time had come to take the test for entry, and like many other tests she took, she passed, and was accepted into the Delayed Entry Program. She would be a member of the U.S. Air Force, and July 14, 1981 would be the day of escape. All she knew, was that this young country girl was going to get to travel the world and make a difference in the lives of many. Finally, her life was moving in a positive direction, or so she thought.

# Part II:
## The Lost Years

*There is a way that appears to be right, but in the end it leads to death.*
*– Proverbs 16:25 (NIV)*

## Back to the Future

She had no idea that the same demons that had plagued her up until high school would be going with her into the military. She hated basic training but completed it as a squad leader.

It wasn't the training itself that she hated so badly, but the military training instructions that she was required to obey. She hated being told what to do, when to do it, where to do it, and how to do it. She resented them for trying to make her adhere to rules, principles, honesty, structure, and discipline. Her heart had decided years ago, after her dad passed, to rebel against authority, and it bothered her that the military had no respect for a decision she felt she rightfully deserved to make.

When the time came for detailing and the selection of her desired home base, she chose to go "back home" to Tinker Air Force base in Del City, Oklahoma, instead of being further away from her people. Shortly after being stationed there, she received her first court martial for her involvement and reporting of a fake robbery at the Bulletin Office, where she was responsible for providing temporary housing for military personnel. In actuality, she had allowed her current boyfriend to enter into the building and take money. She loved him more than she loved her career. She was sentenced to 120 days of hard labor and restricted to the base as a consequence for her actions. She was required to pull nails from a discarded pile of hardwood boards in 3-digit degree weather. Appointed to her station during rush hour, she was made to be a spectacle as multiple cars entered and exited while she "paid her dues" to the government. The consequence of hard work, shame and humiliation would unfortunately not be enough to change her ways.

Shortly after completion of her sentence, she was caught stealing from a Target store off-base, arrested, booked in Midwest City Jail, and given a court hearing date. Because she failed to appear at her appointed court date, her bond was revoked and a warrant for her arrest had been issued. This information was relayed to her Commanding Officer and led to receipt of her second court martial, and a dishonorable discharge from the United States Air Force.

After being escorted off the Air Force base, she was too embarrassed to call her family and ask for help. Therefore, she sought help in the arms of an elderly civilian that didn't love her either, and used her just like everyone else she'd given so much of herself to. He was in need of an apartment, and so, although he was ridiculed and embarrassed for being with her, he knew that she could supply his need. He eventually took her back home once he got what he wanted, and that within itself brought on more feelings of inadequacy.

She was rebellious and never liked the rigidity and compliance of the Air Force, and although she was being kicked out, somehow freedom felt good. Her greatest take-away was the removal of the growth in her mouth that her Mother had spoken of yearly since infancy. She was grateful that the Air Force had detected it during a physical prior to basic training.

†

Upon returning home from the Air Force, she began attending the E.T. Dunlap Center For Higher Education, where she enrolled in classes and took on 12-15 hours per semester. There she received the Evelyn Herron Scholarship for 6 consecutive semesters, landed her on the Dean's honor roll, and was enlisted in the Who's Who Among Students in American Junior Colleges.

She went from one guy to the next, and no sooner after returning to her hometown, she had fallen head over hills in love with a younger guy that she had a crush on in grade school. Lucky her, he only lived right down the street from her. They began seeing each other, and she was sure that they would be together forever. However, his mom had other plans for her son, and did everything she could to sabotage their relationship. It worked, and news of him already having another girlfriend ended their lovefest.

Though that guy was out of the picture, another guy who had showed a romantic interest in her for years during high school, would soon continue his pursuit of her. She felt this guy was the only one who really loved her and desired to truly be with her. They began dating but the feelings were never mutual, for it wasn't him that she loved, it was the dreamy lifestyle that he provided for her. Within a year and only a few months after learning she was pregnant, she moved out of her mother's home and began "living the life" with him in Lynn Lane Apartment Complex; a new upscale apartment admired by many, in an area called Uptown. She gained security and a sense of belonging in knowing that she was a man's lady. She was educated, had a man by her side, and a charming living space. She had completed a total of 72 college credits, and was only one class away to earning a degree in Business Administration, but her progress in school would soon be interrupted by a trip to the hospital to birth her first child. It was the happiest day of her life.

From the outside they appeared to be a prospering, happy couple, but there was far more than what met the eye. They were loan sharks and their drug dealings afforded them anything their flesh desired. Her man was a big commodity in the area to say the least, and she reaped all the perks of being with him. The money that they made was dirty, but the community still envied them for it despite the high cost of their lifestyle. Many were indebted to them, and people would owe them their entire checks before they ever earned it. Friday's were their favorite day of the week, and weekends consisted of social gatherings filled with drugs, sex, and alcohol. Due to her past of sexual abuse, it was hard to have a healthy view of sex itself. Having been inappropriately touched by several trusted men throughout her life, she believed that their actions were punishment for something that she had done wrong yet could never seem to figure out. She had become indifferent and learned how to emotionally detach herself from the acts being performed. Her son's father would suggest the arrangement of orgies in their home, inviting others, including relatives to participate in their demonic activities.

✝

One afternoon, there was a knock at the door. It wasn't unusual to have visitors throughout the day; their drug business was lucrative, and her son's father received packages frequently. It was a colleague with yet another package. She opened the door with a greeting, and he entered with the package and proceeded to walk towards the back room to stash it. Her baby was also in the back, and so she followed behind him. As they walked down the hallway, he asked if her man was at work and she confirmed that he was. In that moment he began unbuckling his pants, and said, "I'm going to take me some". She panicked and in hopes of urging him to leave, she began lying frantically, saying that her son's father would be coming home early. He either didn't buy it or he didn't care, because he proceeded to do what he came to do. He was a big guy and there was no fighting him back. He threw her on the bed with ease and as he pinned her arms behind her back she begged, "*Please*, don't do this!". She glanced over at her baby lying on the bed and attempted to reach over and cover his eyes. She wondered if he somehow knew what was happening to his mother. The entire ordeal was truly demonic. In her pain, she watched her baby bounce while he "took him some".

Everything had happened so quickly. She had been raped many times before as a child, but this was the first time that it actually felt like it. It was the first time that she identified these perverse actions as violations. She thought she had escaped this. She thought this was over. She thought her legacy of abuse had ended. Stuff like this was only supposed to happen to little girls with bad supervision, not to women who finally had it together. These demons had some sort of legal right to her. For everyone who wanted to abuse her, had permission to do it without her direct consent.

The rapist was the biggest drug lord locally and in the surrounding areas. When it came to trafficking, transporting, delivering, and dealing various types of drugs, he was king of the pen. He must have felt entitled to have his way with her, and he had no shame in doing so. When she told her son's father what had happened to her earlier that day, he dismissed it with ease. Business seemed to more important to him than her body being violated.

Before all of this happened, she would cook and clean daily. The house always smelled good when he came home. But, things were changing, and all of her nice gestures were rapidly falling to the wayside. No one cared what had happened to her, and because she refused to remove herself from the situation, she had to find a means of coping with it from within. A relationship that once felt like love and security was turning into strictly business, full of underlying hate, uncertainty, anger and resentment.

Everyone who knew the couple thought he was the best thing that had ever happened to her; "he loves you so much", they would say, but it was all a fallacy.

## Crack and Babies

**B**y the age of 23, shortly after the newness of motherhood had vanished, and after the rape incident with the drug lord, she had hit her first crack cocaine pipe and began using almost every day. She became addicted quickly, and her addiction was the result of many other plagues that consumed her life. She started going into the stash, and that *really* disrupted the household. Her son's father would get mad because she was no longer waiting on him to ration her weekly portion. The wait until Friday had become entirely too long; she needed to use daily in order to numb the pain of the recent past. Having learned from the best, she began taking matters into her own hands and no longer needed him to orchestrate anything. If there wasn't money in the bank she would write "hot checks". She knew how to get what she wanted without his approval and she did just that.

Her drug habit had escalated and attached itself to lies, schemes, drama, manipulation, rationalizations, and justifications; all these things leaned on one another, and the list continued. After only 4-months of using drugs, she had become literally too addicted to care for anyone but herself, and had to leave her newborn child in the care of his dad and grandmother while she was away at a rehabilitation center for 28 days. Sadly, this would be the first of many trips that she would make to a rehab center for her horrible habit.

Upon her return home from rehab, she got high on crack immediately. She wondered if she had lied about her son in rehab, but no, all she said about her son was the truth. It was God that she was lying to; God, herself, and everyone else about what had truly meant more to her at that time. No matter what or how she felt about her son, it didn't stop her from trying to cover up the hurt that had never healed from the inside out. That night she asked herself why she ever had to take that "first hit", and it would take her at least 25 years before she would even come close to accepting the truth and finding the answer. Being in the same environment with the same access was an easy setup for failure. Things would be okay for a short while, but they consistently got worse than they were before. It was a vicious, progressive cycle of demonic chaos.

By the time she discovered that she was pregnant for the second time, her habit was full blown and her lifestyle consisted heavily of money, drugs, gambling, alcohol, orgies and other sexual activities; anything that could make her *more* money to consistently support her habit. For years, the same patterns repeated, just at a higher intensity. Every time a female was brought home to participate in their rendezvous, it was going to cost him whatever she wanted, and he had *better* bring it home. It was as if she was running a business of her own.

When her second son was born, at the time of his birth, she waited a lengthy period of time for his dad to arrive at the hospital, but he never showed. Because her baby needed a name and she needed a ride home, she called trusted family members and they were the ones who gave her a ride, and her son a name.

†

The next three years of her life were treacherous, and involved a turbulent drug rollercoaster ride that often led her in rehab or behind bars. She became a patient of countless psych wards and mental institutions, and her excessive drug usage caused her to hear things, see things, and often think things were crawling on her. She was diagnosed with Paranoia and Schizophrenia, but it was all drug-induced. It's a miracle that the symptoms were never lasting, and that they were only present when drugs were found in her system, which unfortunately, was more often than not.

There were a couple of White boys that came over often to buy and sell drugs, and one particular day, she decided to get into their small truck with them. She knew one of the two, and was sure that they had crack that they were willing to share. She nervously sat in the middle, congestedly sandwiched between them both. As they rode down the curvy roads of the country smoking crack, she learned that the driver had no intent in returning her home to her family. They turned down a dark gravel road that had not a house or light in sight; only the moon shone down into the back of the small truck bed. "I'll tell you what we're finna do", suggested the driver to the passenger, and he shared his vivid and gruesome plans of sexual abuse, torment, and disposal of her body in a field. Initially, she thought he was only kidding, until she seen the look on the passenger's face communicating that she was in deep trouble. She was more familiar with the passenger than the driver, and in fear she tugged on his shirt and begged, "Please, don't let him do this to me! My boys know that I left with you all and they will come looking for me if I don't return home." She was right. The passenger had known her family too well, and to get away with such a thing would be nearly impossible. After a long heated debate between the driver and the passenger, the driver agreed to let her live and angrily scuffled the truck out of the ruts of mud they were bogged down into. He cursed her and threatened the passenger as he sped off in frustration, driving nearly 100 miles within the curves. In less than 3 months, the life of the passenger who saved hers was ended with a bullet-shot wound to the head at a club in her hometown.

†

It didn't matter where she lived, her priorities were out of whack and she saw it with her own eyes during her escape to San Diego, California. She dragged her two boys along with her on this move, leaving their father behind and moving in temporarily with her oldest sister.

One day, her oldest son was hit by a car, while she handled business in a building downtown. He was with her, but had somehow made his way out of the building where they were, crossed the street and was hit as he re-crossed the street to return back into the building where she and her sister had been. He was rushed to the hospital to receive care for his broken bones, and as sad she was for *him*, what she saw in the hospital's Pediatric Ward moved her even greater. Over a thousand newborn babies appeared to be fighting for their lives. All of the children had been awarded to the state and had been displaced and found in dumpsters and abandoned homes. They were connected to

39

machines and feeding tubes, and had no one to call their own. She saw that God *had* been good to her, even while she was running from Him and dragging her kids along.

It was only a matter of time before she would find another love interest and news would reach her sons' father back in her hometown. In a jealous fury, he joined her in San Diego to put out any potential sparks that were flying, and the two of them got an apartment together. Times were hard in San Diego and the cost of living was high. In fact, they would often dumpster dive in search for cans and bottles to recycle, so that they could use the money to purchase dinner for his family. Chicken, potatoes, beans, and "pop" was all that they needed. Family members pitched in the best that they could, sending food stamps and supplies, but they needed more than family could provide.

One morning after dropping her son off at a daycare, which was only across the street from her apartment complex, she fell and broke her ankle. Her neighbors heard her wail as she lay on the ground, and she was rushed in an ambulance to a nearby hospital. She underwent surgery involving the insertion of permanent screws and was eventually discharged. When released from the hospital she made call after to call to find an attorney who could help her get compensation for her injury. She indeed found an attorney, but by the time the case was opened, financial burdens had become unbearable. They were hungry! So, after the attorney agreed to take her case, he gave her small settlement advances, and with it, her and her family returned to her hometown.

She made call after call again to her attorney once she returned home, and he sent paper after paper. It was finally a happy day when she received a settlement larger than expected; a $20,000 check followed by an even larger, $32,000 check. To her surprise, the state deemed her pain and suffering worth the cost of her surgery and opted out of requiring a reimbursement.

Everyone she associated herself with got high. The devil had her so entangled in his trap, that she was literally paying the cost to die a slow death. Although she gave a portion of her money to family out of guilt, within 90 days of receiving her $52,000 settlement, she had exhausted it in entirety and was writing hot checks again. She ran so hard and did so much to numb all she was experiencing. She had no emotions, no sincerity, nor concern for her own well-being. Then, she went to prison!

She sought out temporal things for her own peace of mind instead of eternal things pertaining to her destiny. Any alternative to what she had been taught would suffice, but deep down, she knew, that only Jesus Christ could save her. The peace she sought in the world never fulfilled. It was always contingent on something else, some form of pleasure. She had to give up so much of herself for it.

Although she was accustomed to torment and disorder, ever so often she would find herself going to church, coming as she was, in search of peace, solace and stability. She was there in body, but certainly not in spirit. There were moments where she would enter the church with purses and pockets full of drugs and paraphernalia. She could hardly wait for the services to be over, so that she could go back to her routine of getting high once again. When she approached the altar, she would keep her hands in her pocket to ensure that that her crack pipe didn't fall on the floor. The devil thought he had her, and he did; she was living for him and he was using her in attempt to mock God.

† 

Because of her loose, drug-infested lifestyle, by the time she had gotten pregnant the third time, she wondered about the father of this child, and didn't know until the day he was born, when she saw that he looked exactly like his older brother. Similar to her pregnancy with her second son, she smoked crack cocaine nearly up until the day he was born, and his system was full of it at the time of his birth. Nonetheless, the hospital staff allowed her to take her baby home with Mother, and had no inquiries regarding her drug usage.

Immediately upon leaving the hospital, she left her newborn baby with his aunt for two days so she could catch up on her drug escapades and orgies with their dad and other ladies. The two of them picked cousins from both sides of their family to smoke crack and perform sexual favors. The drugs, money, jewelry, pornography, stealing, gambling, men, women, lying, scheming, manipulation, justifications, and all the other things that consumed her life were her primary focus. They took precedence over all, including her three children. Everything that she said she wouldn't do, she had done.

By early Monday morning, someone from both the hospital and the health department had arrived at her home with a delivery of 24 cans of baby formula milk, along with some kind of medicine for the baby. It was obvious that they knew something was wrong with him, and this was their unethical way of dealing with it.

✝

In one of many moments, smoke filled a motel room as her three sons laid on a blanket placed on the floor; the youngest still in diapers. She smoked crack and got high for several hours with several different people. At the seventh hour, there finally came a knock on the door. Her stomach sunk in dreaded fear that the knock was for her. When the guy answering the door looked in the peephole, he froze, and in that moment she was certain that the knock *was* for her. It was Mother and her younger brother who happened to be a Police Officer in her hometown. She was so afraid to face them and their reaction, but all Mother did was look at her sternly and say, "Give me the keys to the car and my grandbabies!" Her younger brother, however, wanted to fight everyone in the room except her. That evening, the two of them returned her home without her boys, and when the door closed behind her, the feeling of worthlessness and hopelessness rushed over her. Unfortunately, it still wasn't enough to keep her from getting high again the next day.

✝

One night, she took a ride with her sister's fiancé, and it was a night she would never forget. He raped her. It was a drug-related incident, like most were, but it was a violation nonetheless. He had just received a package of crack that night and had looked at her, flashed the package and asked, "Sister-in-law, you want to ride with me?". In thinking he would provide her with more crack for her habit, she agreed and he informed her son's father, "Man, she gon' ride with me". They rode into the dark of the night down a dirt road and eventually pulled over and parked. In that sinister moment, he turned to her and said, "I'm fince to take me some". She had heard similar words before and was in fear and disbelief. Her face must have shown it, because no sooner had he replied, "You think I'm playing…". Fear numbed her, and he tore her up sexually as she wept. She glanced towards the house nearby; she was so close to safety, yet so far away. He placed his brawly hand on one of his big rifles, looked at her intimidatingly, and said "You bet' not holler". That night, she thought she would surely die.

She later revealed to her sister, that the man she was planning to marry had raped her. Whether or not her sister believed her, the couple proceeded with their wedding plans, things were swept under the rug, and *she* had ironically agreed to be a member of their wedding party, and even enlisted her youngest son as the ring bearer.

✝

The time had come in the cycle to leave home again, but this time she was going to prison at the Dr. Eddie Warrior Correctional Center. She was sentenced to Fort Female Offenders Regiment Training for several charges to include, possession of controlled substance and shoplifting. Her time in prison brought back so many hurting pains and desperate emotions. During this time her country had experienced a terrorist bombing attack in Oklahoma City that left 168 people dead, and her hopeless in a cell. She was really beginning to hate herself.

In attempt to escape reality, she was in and out of the home frequently, and her two boys got used to visiting their mom in some facility she had landed herself in. She would manipulate with great emotion and tears to ensure their father would bring them to see her and adhere to their visiting schedule. Jail and rehab had ashamedly become a place of comfort for her. It was a dysfunctional yet familiar routine that was easy to follow, and as the years went on and her habit progressed, others became familiar with the routine as well.

She was now fully supporting her own habit and doing the same things she hated her sons' father for. Although her boys loved her, they resented her for abandoning them, and she found it hard to believe that they could ever love a mother who was in and out of their life the way that she was.

She just couldn't be still and always had to be going somewhere or doing something. Silence and stillness were torture. She would leave walking down dark country roads unable to see her hand in front of her face, and that seemed appropriate. What did it matter if she died or placed herself in harm's way? The way life was going, it seemed that could be the best thing that would ever happen to her. All Mother could do was advise her that when she left her house, to at least slow down when leaving so that Mother could identify the vehicle she drove off in, in the event she never returned and had to go looking for her.

†

There was a millionaire in her hometown, and she was sure to befriend him. She took a trip with him once to a hotel and casino in Louisiana from her hometown, and boy, what a time they had! Although it was late, cold and dark, she was bold and fearless and would steal his truck and proceed to walk across the railroad tracks alone to purchase drugs from a group of foreign drug dealers. She had plenty of money to pay for the drugs, for she stole his wallet full of hundreds of dollars after getting him drunk and high on dope. Night after night she persisted until finally the group of drug dealers became suspicious about the source of her money and implied she may have been undercover.

After three full days of roaming around, drugging, and doing all sorts of dark activities, they had made it as far back as Texarkana from Louisiana. She was exhausted, couldn't go on any further, and all she could think about was dying. Paranoia had set in and she was psychotic with fear and severe trembles. It was the most out of her mind that she had ever been. With the very little sense that she had left, she called Mother and informed her that she was somewhere near the state line in Texarkana. In less than 30 minutes it seemed, Mother, one of her brothers, along with her sons and some nieces and nephews, would come to her rescue, finding her in yet *another* motel room.

Time passed, and in 1998, Mother had become very ill and suffered a stroke. Mother was in a hospital intensive care unit, and it was no surprise that she was in a drug recovery facility at the time Mother needed her most. She was released to visit Mother while she was on her death bed. During her visit, she climbed in the bed with Mother and whispered in her ear. She began asking her for forgiveness for not being there for her when she needed her most, and forgiveness for being disobedient to her wise instructions over the years. She told Mother to squeeze her hand if she could understand what she was saying. She looked up to see if Mother was responding, and a tear had fallen down her cheek. As she touched her face to wipe her tears away with one hand, Mother squeezed her other hand. Although Mother spoke no words, the squeeze of Mother's hand communicated forgiveness and gave a sense of relief.

As she left that day to return to the rehab facility, she received a call while en route, that her precious Mother had died. She was later excused again to attend Mother's funeral. It saddened her that she couldn't give Mother a parting gift of sobriety if she wanted to, and the pain of Mother's death didn't help her reach it either. It would also be years before she could every truly receive her Mother's grace.

✝

Only a few years later, she was arrested and charged with grand larceny from a retailer for stealing over $50 worth of merchandise. During her court hearing, the judge decided to combine her previous charges of petty larcenies with her current charge, and so, she was sentenced to prison again at Dr. Eddie Warrior Correctional Center. She flipped out in a dramatic rage in the courtroom, but her sentence remained. In prison, the news broadcasting aired yet another terrorist attack on her country in the state of New York, destroying the twin towers and wiping out countless lives. As she sat and tutored women within the prison, they watched one plane after another crash into the twin towers. The entire incident left her feeling helpless, hopeless, sad, lonely, and crushed. She longed to be with her family, friends, and loved ones.

Within three years of being out of a prison, her lifestyle had booked her in county jail yet again. Her cell was directly next to the door to the exercise court. Every morning, she would hear a young man singing and praising God. She became drawn to the daily experience and his infectious voice became her daybreak alarm clock. She would repeat his prayers back to the other ladies that were awake with her at the time, and they too were intrigued. They were in awe because his prayers were not for freedom to get back on the outside, but he prayed to find freedom on the inside while he waited to go to prison. They would try to talk to him through the cracks of the door, and request that he re-sing the last song he sung.

To her surprise, on day 52, the bailiff opened the door to her cell and casually said, "go home". She would be out of jail only three days before receiving news that her younger brother had been killed. The recollection of prayers and praises from jail's exercise court helped her accept her younger brother's death. The songs rang within her. Sadly, in that moment, jail seemed like a safer place.

†

While living and working part-time in an apartment complex owned by an ill and elderly woman in Muskogee, Oklahoma, she received the opportunity for another escape once the woman passed away. The woman's brother visited to assist his sister, and interim he requested her assistance, and offered her a severance pay in exchange.

She was leaving Oklahoma again, but this time to live in the state of Maine, only a few miles from the Canadian border. It seemed she was the only black person in the entire state; a minority to say the least. One day, while working, she met a wealthy, white-haired elderly woman. "There must be a God in Heaven!", the woman said, as she called her over to her table, touched her hands, and looked into her eyes. In the woman's 76 years of life, she had never been in eyesight proximity of a Black person. The two of them became friends and shared many hours of conversation. She sat with her often while the woman drank her morning coffee with breakfast. The woman would ask her many questions like, "How in the world did you end up here? And, she would answer. Each day, she would tell the woman more and more about herself, and they swapped stories. The woman shared about her children, her estate, and her reasons for being intrigued by her.

Her and her new friend had learned a lot from each other and shed tears of sadness together when it was time for her to return to her hometown. The woman was right, only a God in heaven could have arranged such a beautiful friendship.

One morning, there laid a letter on her pillow addressed to her from the elderly man she had been caring for. "Just read it, Andrea!", he insisted. And in it, he informed her that she must return home. It read that he would cover the expenses to send her home, just as he had covered the expenses to bring her there. She had already nearly depleted his life savings, and even then, he was willing to offer her more.

†

Her return home didn't last long. The negative thoughts of her chaotic life in shambles had caused her to leave again in search of something to fill the deep, dark void within her soul, and lift her out of her pit of despair. No matter how many times she tried on her own to stop doing all of the evil things that she was involved in, she just didn't have the strength to stop completely. She got so sick and tired of going back and forth into jails, prisons, mental institutions, rehabs, homes, behavioral health centers, etc., only to return to be pushed down again from the top of a slippery slide leading to destruction. She knew that her life was coming to a dead-end halt without fulfilling her purpose, and the foreshadowing of that reality saddened her. If that happened, there would be another failure to add to her record.

She checked herself into a domestic violence center called Women In Safe Home (WISH) in Muskogee, Oklahoma. Her stay at WISH only lasted a short while before she was checked into a motel room and up to her dealing habits again. There she would live for months, paying for her motel stays by the week, as she ran a business selling prescription narcotics. She met with clients regularly, and rationed out her monthly prescriptions amongst them. Some would buy, and some would trade. At the end of her "shifts", when she was alone in her thoughts, she would sometimes call the local crisis center. She never told them who she was, but she would tell them that she wasn't from there, that she was smoking drugs, picking at her skin horribly, and contemplating suicide. Although she contemplated suicide, she feared lying down, and thought if she did she would not wake up. During her phone conversations she would tell them that "they" were listening. She didn't know who "they" were, but Paranoia had convinced her that "they" could hear their conversation, and the bath tub was the only safe enclosure. After the third or fourth call to the crisis center, she was identified, and asked, "Is your name Andrea Grayson? Your people are looking for you." Fear came over her, and she knew she had to escape.

She checked out of the motel and slept in the home of anyone who would allow her. She risked her life and it landed her in the hands of drug dealers, rapists, thieves and murderers.

Whenever she was sexually abused by a man who happened to be in a relationship, she was sure to inform their female partner about what their man had done to her. Almost always, the women lacked sympathy and would be angry at *her*, blaming her for her promiscuous, drug-infested lifestyle that she lived. They may have been right, but even the worst of women didn't deserve to be violated.

Not knowing who to call or cry her heart out to, she called her youngest son and informed him that she had been raped in Muskogee, Oklahoma. He asked many questions in bewilderment, and just wanted to know why his mother couldn't come home.

Finally, her whereabouts had been leaked to her older sister by one of her former clients who happened to be a Pastor's wife in the area. By the time her older sister had come and found her in Muskogee, she was psychotic and out of her mind. When found, she was wearing a blue, long-sleeved wool coat in the heat of the Summer. Although a part of her wanted to keep running, she was happy to be found.

The look on her sister's face when she saw her was one of disbelief. Her sister had told her that she was going to call their brother who lived in California. They were close, and she knew that if she told him, he would surely come and put an end to all of this like he did when they were kids. She listened as her sister spoke to her brother on the phone: "If we ever had to wonder if she needs help, we don't have to wonder anymore. We have to help her now, or she's going to die out here in these streets. If only you could see her, you would know that she's really sick."

In little time, her brother had flown to Oklahoma to take her back to California with him. Once again, her family came to her rescue. He was the Mordecai to the Esther within her, and she had been given another opportunity to live.

Almost immediately after arriving in California, she joined a women's rehab home where she became sober, made great progress, and was eventually entrusted with a leadership position; overseeing other women like herself within the home. Despite her progress, eight months later she would receive a phone call sharing the news that her youngest son was involved in a shooting incident and was being charged as an adult. The call grieved her greatly and the news impeded her thoughts, initiating a return back to her hometown yet again, 2 months later.

While in the women's recovery home she met a guy from the men's home who shortly made arrangements to meet her in her hometown via bus. Although the two of them were broken and still in need of much help, they strived to be together and forge a romantic relationship. The two of them quickly reverted back to their former worldly way of living, indulging themselves in drugs and alcohol. It was a horrible situation, and the guy eventually returned to San Diego.

One day while doing hair, she was introduced to her client's male cousin who expressed interest in her quickly. When he met her he told her he was going to marry her; she blushed.

Seeing that he was in drug court, and acknowledging that she would have to be drug-free to be with him and satisfy the courts, she checked herself into the Dallas, TX women's rehab home under the same organization as the last home she went to in San Diego. Her old habits did not die easily. While at the women's recovery home in Dallas, she went back and forth to her hometown every third weekend of each month to get her monthly prescriptions and make arrangements for them to be sold while away. The recovery home noticed her traveling trend and attempted to put an end to it.

Her new beau caused her self-esteem to sky-rocket like never before, and he was certainly a great motivation to return back home. They spoke often while she was in Dallas and he urged her to come and be his wife. Although he had controlling and possessive ways, she became infatuated with him and made the move with haste. The one and only time she was ever married was to him, and it lasted for less than 90 days. Because she lacked love for herself, she did all she could to ensure that someone else would love her the way that she hadn't. Even through her hurt and pain, she had to come to grips of his reasoning for ending the marriage suddenly. He had told her many things about his childhood, much of which she concluded, he never properly healed from. And for these same childhood reasons, he could not remain married to her. Although he was the love of her life, he felt she was almost too good for him and doubted that their relationship could be true love. He said that she had many of the same characteristics of his mother and he never wanted to see his mother hurt. Her husband told her she was the best thing to ever happen to him, but he knew he wasn't good for her. Not long after, he decided to get an annulment and returned her back home, only a short distance away. He said that he didn't want to hurt her any more than she already was. At least this time, her discharge was honorable.

When we're not healed from the inside out, we seek pleasure in people, places, and things.

We seek happiness in the world outside of ourselves, and we long for a relationship to make us feel whole. Whether her marriage lasted or ended, it didn't matter. She wasn't healed and marriage could never be the solution to her problems; Jesus Christ was the answer.

### Fork in the Road

Ill-decision making seemed to be a lifelong trend for her, and she had placed herself in danger yet again while leaving Choctaw Casino in Idabel, Oklahoma. She chose to get a ride home in a car with a family she had never met. Though she gave the male driver directions instructing him where to turn, he instead continued to drive miles and miles into darkness alone on a county road, leading them somewhere near Dangerfield, Texas, and it felt like danger! He held her in a small trailer house filled with lots of people of all ages, from infants to senior citizens. She was being badly mistreated by him and held there against her will. The mistreatment was so poor, that his mom would beg, "please let this girl go back home to her family!"

On the third day of kidnapping, the son had left the house momentarily, and his mother had compassion for her and allowed her to call her older sister. Her sister called her cousin to pick her up, and he did. For some reason God kept saving her life, and it would take years before she ever understood why He just wouldn't let her die in her mess.

# FOR SUCH A TIME AS THIS

✝

The pit she was in was cold, dark and lonely. She felt empty and didn't want to live anymore and so, she had struck a deal with the devil that she would kill herself. After being up late one night at her son's house, she waited for him to go to sleep. When she heard him snoring, she grabbed the keys to his truck, and a shoe box filled with all of the money that she could find in his house. She hopped in his truck, turned the key, and changed the radio station from rambunctious rap to uplifting gospel, as was her custom, and proceeded to drive.

She was going to drive into the Red River bridge that crossed over from Oklahoma to Texas, and drown herself, the money, and his truck. With those treasures of her son's missing, she thought there would be no remnants of that demonic lifestyle left for him to grasp onto. She couldn't help herself, but maybe before she was gone, she could somehow help him.

Without remorse, she decided to first stop at the casino and gamble some of the money she had stolen. It was her last day and last hoorah and so she gambled for her last time. As time went by, she repeatedly glanced down at her watch, for her and the devil had decided that she needed to leave the casino no later than 9 a.m. if she was going to keep her early appointment with death. If she and the devil were going to do this, there was no room for error and she would have to be strategic. She would drive really fast toward the Red River; at least 150 mph. It had to be fast enough to go over the rail, because crashing into the rail would result in a failed attempt, and her potentially living. As she drove, the brightness of the sun glared in her face. A moment of despair and demise was not supposed to be bright. Something so celestial and beautiful was annoyingly shining on a heart so dark and ugly. In that moment, a gospel song of encouragement titled "Open My Heart" played on the radio. As the artist sung, tears she thought no longer existed rolled down her face. The Lord himself was interceding for her with a song.

She wiped her tears in anger at the realization that her suicide plans were being destroyed. Her heart had been pricked by the words in the song and all she kept saying was, "Lord, I don't want to live like this anymore. I can't keep making the same mistakes over and over again!" In her moment of contrite brokenness, she had somehow passed the Red River, and it was now behind her. She wanted to leave this world, but she was desperately afraid to die in sin. She proposed to God, "If I truly have a purpose in life, let me fulfill it without wavering; lead me where *You* would have me to go". It was like God began driving the truck that day and telling her to get out of the way and let Him have all of her, so that like in the song, she would no longer have to make the same mistakes over and over again. The devil and The Lord fought for her that day and the Lord had won. Truthfully, He won long ago on the cross when He hung His head and declared "It is finished". That day, her old self died in a way that she couldn't have imagined. She had chosen life at the brink of death, but she was going to need God's help in serving Him.

Even after making the right decision she felt horrible. How could this be? The devil was clearly upset and tormented her with feelings of cowardness for not following through with her plans. She had breached their contract and unclenched his hold. All she had to do was kill herself, and she couldn't even do *that* right.

Instead of drowning in the river, she ended up driving to a hospital in Texarkana to visit her son's girlfriend and mother of her grandsons who was in the hospital for another time due to an ongoing illness. She stayed in the hospital with her by her side for 8 days as she watched her fight for her will to live. Although to the hospital she was but a visitor, it felt like the two of them were hospitalized together. She was with the daughter she never had, and being there for her somehow helped her find purpose in fighting for her own life; they had escaped death together in different ways, and gratitude filled her heart. She was discovering that she had to die to herself so that others could live. Though everyone she could think of was upset with her, having learned of her truck and money theft, this was the start of a new beginning!

†

Nearly the entire town was still bitter towards her for her recent acts of thievery, and there were few places she could go and be welcomed. Her son had always been a man of few words, but during this time, his words were even fewer after hearing her explanation for having to leave again. After her return to her hometown, she had plans to leave her son's home and head to the SOS Battered Women's Shelter. Over a period of days, she began cleaning out the room where she housed all of her junk, and preparing for yet another leave. Even after admittance into SOS, she went back and forth to her son's home. She was at her son's house by day, and at SOS by night, striving to stay clean in her own strength.

In conversation with her sister, she was reminded and advised to contact a free rehab facility she had once been admitted to in another state. They had various locations throughout the United States, and the nearest to her was one in Fort Worth. For 7 days her and her sister called and got the run-around before reaching someone who could finally help her. She was allowed to arrive on a Monday, but family ties were strong and kept her a day longer than expected. It was like she was being held hostage by her son who didn't want his mother to leave, again! He urged her not to do it, but she knew it was necessary. Even after all she had put her son through, he wanted his mom to stay home, and repeatedly asked why she had to leave. He bargained that she should at least stay for the sake of her grandchildren. But all she could think of was how close she came to death only days earlier, and how backing out of her plans to leave, would surely lead to a tragic end.

Finally, she arranged for her baby brother to pick her up early Tuesday morning before anyone would wake, for her next escape without goodbyes. It was a life or death decision, and she had chosen life.

✝

Those in the facility in Fort Worth didn't favor her a bit. In fact, she was treated very poorly, but she figured almost anything was better than her former life. It was a 6-month program, but she was asked to leave after 5 ½ months for unknown reasons. Despite the mistreatment, she took all of the knowledge positive tools and lessons with her to her new residence with the mother of her brother's children.

She eventually found refuge at Southside Church in Fort Worth, Texas. They represented Jesus well there, and welcomed her like the prodigal child that she was. Their arms were open and God used them to lift her out of despair and hopelessness.

# Part III:
## *The Process*

*No weapon that is formed against you will prosper;*
*And every tongue that accuses you in judgment you*
*will condemn. This is the heritage of the servants of*
*the Lord, And their vindication is from Me." declares*
*the Lord.*
*— Isaiah 54:17 (NASB)*

## Truth Be Told

For years she was so angry with God. She blamed Him for everything bad that had happened in her life, and for every wrong choice *she* had made. Her flesh hated the very idea of Him and His Word, and because it did, she lived a life of rebellion, turning her back on every good thing she had ever been taught as a child. The hurt and pain of life had hardened her heart, and she had become a bitter person.

Regardless of all of the times she was in and out of drug rehabs, behavior health facilities, jails, and prisons over the years, and regardless of all of the times that she'd prayed and asked God to take away certain destructive habits and behaviors, He wouldn't take away a single thing! In the many moments she was too weak to fight, she still had a strong will that wouldn't surrender all. She was comfortable in her mess and had held onto all of it with a tight grip. One day, God spoke to her and said, "As much as I want to take them away from you, I won't do it until you give them to *Me*, then, they will no longer be yours." He was such a gentleman, and although He wanted all of her, He wasn't forceful like the men of her past. He didn't want bits and pieces, or even a large percentage. He paid a price for *all* of her, and *all* was what He wanted. Until she was ready to give Him *that* and completely surrender, He wouldn't take a single ailment away. Walking with God was proving to be much more difficult than running from Him. If she was going to allow Him to heal her, the truth about her and the life she had lived would have to be told; to her *first*.

*But he said to me, "My grace is sufficient for you, for my power is made perfect in weakness." Therefore I will boast all the more gladly about my weaknesses, so that Christ's power may rest on me.*
*– 2 Corinthians 12:9 (NIV)*

Due to the inability to accurately identify and cope with her emotions, she grew accustomed to making excuses for her negative behavioral patterns. Throughout the years she had learned to express emotional pain through self-harm, and it would certainly require a transformation and renewal of her mind to be able to view her past in any other way but falsely. She had to admit that she was weak, and she needed God's strength to do even that. Only He could guide her into all truth and identify the reasons for the mess of her past.

*But when he, the Spirit of truth, comes, he will guide you into all the truth...*
*– John 16:13 (NIV)*

In order to heal from past hurts, hang-ups, and habits that were killing her and keeping her sick, she had to make the choice to be vulnerable. Sharing her dirty secrets unlocked the door of shame and guilt and uncovered the mask of pride that she'd worn for so long. When she masked her pain and stuffed her emotions, she was only hiding from herself. She had to stop making excuses for her poor behavior. No more, "My daddy died!", "I'm hurt!", "I'm angry!", "I got raped!", "I'm lonely!", "I'm hungry!", "I was molested!", "I'm tired!", "I was used!", "I was abused!", "I'm broken!", "I'm mad!", "You talked about me!", "That's just how I am!". Every single excuse had to be eliminated, dismissed from the poll and ejected from the election.

*Come to me, all you who are weary and burdened,*
*and I will give you rest.*
*– Matthew 11:28 (NIV)*

Grieving the past was the hardest of it all. She grieved both the things she hated and the things she loved, but hated to let go. She cried for 18 months straight, and all the tears that fell were necessary and flowed from the inside out. She would wake daily and tell herself, "I'm not crying today. I'm sick of being a cry baby!", and then the tears would fall again. She was so used to living a life of deception that kept her numb to the truth. There was so much inside of her that she had never felt and properly grieved, and the tears had to fall in order to bring about healing in every aspect, especially for the wounded child inside. The little girl within her sobbed, the young woman within her cried, and the maturing woman of God wept for the both of them.

*He heals the brokenhearted and binds up their wounds.*
*– Psalm 147:3 (NIV)*

Until she could accept the truth regarding all of the addictions, she would never be able to accept her salvation. She realized that her sobriety and her salvation were contingent upon one another. She developed an "all or nothing" mentality; if it negatively affected her sobriety, then it negatively affected her salvation. For all the times she lied, stole, cheated, manipulated, justified, rationalized, ostracized, blamed, shamed, fornicated, committed adultery, lived in fear, engaged in lesbianism affairs, gotten drunk, gotten high, felt superior or inferior, wallowed in false-guilt, loathed in unforgiveness, judged, back-stabbed, belittled, used others, became engulfed in pornography, indulged in debauchery, dabbled in witchcraft, wanted to kill herself, lived for the world and fulfilled fleshly desires. For all of the nights she stayed up drinking, drugging, gambling, partying, not loving God, not loving herself, and not loving others; for *all* of these reasons *and more*, Jesus Christ had died on the cross. She couldn't help but be brokenhearted by the truth about her, and be overwhelmed by the truth about her Savior.

During a stay at an upscale behavioral health facility, she encountered a prestigious Certified Drug and Alcohol Counselor. He had worked there for over 17 years and boasted about his hourly pay. He spewed out his respected opinions concerning her and other patients in group settings with several different people in attendance. On one particular day, the words he vomited in arrogance, shattered her heart and damaged her self-esteem even further than its present state. In relation to her circumstance and in light of her recovery process, he told her that she would always be institutionalized and that she would never be able to live a productive life in society. She received and believed his words, so they stuck with her for many years. She figured he of course knew what he was talking about, and his credentials earned him the right to speak in to her life. Little did she know, God would prove him to be a liar, and offer her hope for eternity, free of charge.

## Finding Peace

The very day that she was honest with God about how she felt about Him, and asked Him for forgiveness, is the very day that she was able to rest in His loving arms! He didn't hold anything against her, nor did He shame her for believing lies and feeling a sense of abandonment and hate towards Him. He loved her even when she couldn't love herself *or* Him.

She surely identified with the immoral woman in the bible who wiped her tears from Jesus' feet with her hair. The woman's alabaster jar filled with expensive perfume meant nothing to her, as she anointed the feet of her Savior.

*"For this reason I say to you, her sins, which are many, have been forgiven, for she loved much; but he who is forgiven little, loves little." Then He said to her, "Your sins have been forgiven."*
*– Luke 7:47 & 48 (ESV)*

There was a game called tug-of-war that she occasionally played as a child, which had now enlightened her understanding of forgiveness. In the game, as long as the parties on each end of the rope were tugging, there was indeed a war. If someone let go of the rope, however, the war was over. Forgiving many allowed her to let go of her end of the rope. No matter how hard others tugged at the other end, releasing them ended the war.

Unforgiveness is like an invisible umbilical cord that connects us to those we haven't forgiven. Although the life events that caused us to harbor ill feelings toward others may have occurred long ago, until we forgive them, we are still connected. People will indefinitely do things that hurt and upset us, and it is far too easy to collect offenses on behalf of those we love. Some of those people may even be dead, but our lack of forgiveness keeps us attached and stifled until the moment we set ourselves free by forgiving. Jesus teaches us to ask God daily for forgiveness and extend forgiveness daily to those who have sinned against us. It is a daily prayer, for a daily occurrence.

*For if you forgive other people when they sin against you, your heavenly Father will also forgive you.*
*– Matthew 6:14 (NIV)*

True forgiveness meant dropping the charges off of everyone who had harmed her in any way. She no longer wanted to be the victim or make justifications that left her complacent. In forgiving those who abused her, she could no longer use their abuse as an excuse to use drugs. She could no longer point the finger at anyone, including herself, because forgiveness put her finger down. She chose to go all the way back and forgive as much evil things as she could remember. It took more strength to let go, than it did to hold on.

*Create in me a clean heart, O God. Renew a loyal spirit within me.*
*— Psalm 51:10 (NLT)*

The lifestyle she lived had shunned her from society, and she really couldn't blame those who did. The one and only thing that could remove the shame and guilt that loomed over her and give her a clean conscience would be the divine forgiveness of God.

She began learning more and more daily how the decisions she made shaped her destiny, and how love didn't exist where there was no free will to choose. Her past choices had landed her in jail cells, drug rehabilitations, dope houses, defiled marriage beds, and the list goes on and on. She felt banished from the presence of the Lord, and being far away from Him was no fun place to be. She compared her numerous years of separation from the Lord to biblical Jonah's time spent in the belly of the whale. For so long her motto was, "What's love got to do with it?", and now, she sees that there's no life without it.

*If I speak in the tongues of men or of angels, but do not
have love, I am only a resounding gong or a clanging
cymbal. If I have the gift of prophecy and can fathom
all mysteries and all knowledge, and if I have a
faith that can move mountains, but do not have love, I
am nothing. If I give all I possess to the poor and give
over my body to hardship that I may boast, but do not
have love, I gain nothing.
– 1 Corinthians 13: 1-3 (NIV)*

She had spent so many years searching for
peace while in fear. "Well, if I've done
something wrong, please forgive me", is what
she often said; all while knowing that she was
falling short of what God truly desired and
required of her. Regardless of the many years
she spent in the "belly of the whale", God's
patience never ran out. His love for her was
relentlessly unconditional and extended beyond
her faults. On the rare occasions she felt her
past was no one's business, she remembered the
love of Her Father, and eagerly re-surrendered it
all and obeyed His Holy Spirit to tell her story.

*And I am convinced that nothing can ever separate us from God's love. Neither death nor life, neither angels nor demons, neither our fears for today nor our worries about tomorrow—not even the powers of hell can separate us from God's love. No power in the sky above or in the earth below—indeed, nothing in all creation will ever be able to separate us from the love of God that is revealed in Christ Jesus our Lord.*
*– Romans 8:38 & 39 (NLT)*

Too often she had been urged to, "Just let it go and move on!", but in order to do that, she had to understand that all of the experiences she held onto mattered. The molestation, the deaths, the rapes, the sexual identity crisis, the hurts, the pains, the habits, the complexes. All of these things mattered to Satan, for they were the very things he used to keep her in bondage. He used them to make her feel guilty, to make her feel afraid, to make her feel abandoned, sad and depressed. He vaulted her deepest darkest secrets within her and helped her justify her self-destructive lifestyle almost to the point of suicide.

When she opened her eyes to the truth, opened her heart to forgiveness, and began believing every word written in The Holy Bible, then and only then did she began to understand why so many things had happened to her. This gave her peace, and the courage to move on with life.

> *The unfolding of your words gives light; it gives understanding to the simple.*
> *– Psalm 119:130 (NIV)*

What is needed is true confession, repentance, and asking of forgiveness for what we specifically have done wrong. This acknowledgement tells God how sincere we are about our walk with Him. Once we have confessed and asked for forgiveness, we must accept His grace and receive it by faith; we are then forgiven. There is never a need to feel shamed or condemned. When Jesus died for our sins, He took on our punishment. Often times we have a tendency to want justice for others and grace for ourselves. It doesn't work that way. We will all be judged by God in the same manner and with the same standard that we judge others; grace for grace, justice for justice, and mercy for mercy.

> *Therefore, there is now no condemnation for those who are in Christ Jesus, because through Christ Jesus the law of the Spirit who gives life has set you free from the law of sin and death.*
> *– Romans 8:1-2 (NIV)*

Obeying God by praying blessings over those who have offended us allows our thoughts and feelings toward them to change. He is faithful to heal our emotions so that we can move forward with renewed hearts. As we bless others, He blesses us.

*But to you who are listening I say: Love your enemies, do good to those who hate you, bless those who curse you, pray for those who mistreat you.*
*– Luke 6:27-28 (NIV)*

No longer was the validation of another required. No one had to tell her who she was or make her feel good about herself, or reach her something that they could potentially snatch back. No one even had to apologize. No, she had found a new identity. She found something, or Someone, rather, that the world didn't give, so the world couldn't take away.

She realized that her situation wasn't unique at all. She was a sinner, and sinning was a common ailment of mankind; a way of human nature. Whether her past decisions were right or wrong, they meant absolutely nothing at the foot of the cross. All that mattered was her willingness to move on in Christ and trust His miraculous plan for her life.

*For I know the plans I have for you," declares the LORD, "plans to prosper you and not to harm you, plans to give you hope and a future.*
*– Jeremiah 29:11 (NIV)*

God doesn't promise to give us a painless way of life. He promises a way of escape. He promises to help us bear the pain and to give us strength to get back on our feet when our own weaknesses cause us to stumble.

*Beloved, think it not strange concerning the fiery trial which is to try you, as though some strange thing happened unto you: But rejoice, inasmuch as ye are partakers of Christ's sufferings; that, when his glory shall be revealed, ye may be glad also with exceeding joy.*
*– 1 Peter 4:12- (KJV)*

## Happier Even After

She accepted Jesus Christ as her Savior at a very young age. Nonetheless, for years she ran hard and fast trying to get away from the designed purpose He had for her life. Wherever she went and no matter what she was doing, grace caught up with her, and Jesus was there. She took Him in the darkest of places and betrayed His trust, but He still remained in love with her and shone His light. She proudly displayed her feeble knowledge, yet He still boldly blessed her with His divine wisdom. When she ran long enough and stood at death's door, He went before her, conquered it, and said, "It is finished" before she could say it and take her own life.

Even in the midst of darkness she rebuked the enemy. Prior to taking hits of crack, she would often say aloud, "This too shall pass", and many former drug colleagues would reflect on how she preached, even in the crack houses they rummaged through. She had broken every promise she had made to God, yet He never changed His mind about her. She had backslid time and time again, yet He remained faithfully married to her, never once breaking His covenant. She was best off being "cold" and ignorant or "hot" and committed, rather than being dangerously lukewarm; lacking reverence for a God that she knew always existed.

*I know your deeds, that you are neither cold nor hot. I wish you were either one or the other! So, because you are lukewarm—neither hot nor cold—I am about to spit you out of my mouth.*
*– Revelation 3:15-17 (NIV)*

The question she had to answer was not "*Will* I bow down to God?", and "*Will* I confess?", but, "*When* will I bow down to God?", and "*When* will I confess?". She had decided that it would be sooner rather than later.

*It is written: "'As surely as I live,' says the Lord, 'every knee will bow before me; every tongue will acknowledge God.'"*
*– Romans 14:11 (NIV)*

✝

When babies first start walking, they take unstable steps and reach out for their parents to catch them when they fall. That is the same way her new walk with Christ began. Until her spiritual muscles strengthened, she would continuously fall, and the prayers of loved ones would continuously lift her up. Their prayers, in the name of Jesus, would allow her a fighting chance of receiving a miracle of life again.

*...The prayer of a righteous person is powerful and effective.*
*— James 5:16 (NIV)*

She would be deceiving others if she attributed her deliverance to man. For decades, counseling, rehab facilities, and group meetings would help her only temporarily, but true deliverance would come from her Heavenly Father. Her healing did not come through a pill, a bottle, nor was it written out on man's prescription pad. Only in Jesus Christ was her healing paid for in full; He was the only way. Only by the washing away of her sins with the blood of Jesus Christ, the acceptance of His grace, and the transformation of her heart and mind could she truly be set free. The choice to remain free, however, would be a daily one.

*Jesus answered, "I am the way and the truth and the life. No one comes to the Father except through me...".*
*— John 14:6 (NIV)*

There is a difference in being saved and being delivered. God saved her when she accepted the fact that He sent His Son to die on the cross for her. God saved her when she believed and confessed that Jesus Christ rose from the dead, and is seated today at the right hand of The Father in Heaven. Salvation was free. Her deliverance, however came with a cost.

"At least God knows my heart", is what she would say. But it was only an excuse to dismiss her negative behaviors and keep hold of her life. Now she knew that she had to surrender her life in entirety if she wanted to be set free. She had to surrender her choices, her attitudes, her behaviors, her hurts, her hang-ups, her habits. Deliverance cost her everything.

*For whoever wants to save their life will lose it, but whoever loses their life for me will save it.*
*– Luke 9:24 (NIV)*

The words of her earthly father about her Heavenly Father were finally appearing to be true. Not a single hopeless night of her past was in vain. Every painful ordeal she had experienced *was* for her good and the good of those like her that surrounded her. As she healed and found peace, all that the enemy had meant for her harm was turning around, and it seemed the turmoil he put her through was all a dream. As she moved forward and grew in Christ, she was no longer forced to live in survival mode or settle for temporary solutions to life issues. The devil behind her became smaller and smaller and he can't touch her, for her life is no longer her own, it now belongs to Christ.

*For it is by grace you have been saved, through faith
—and this is not from yourselves, it is the gift of God.
— Ephesians 2:8 (NIV)*

The more of her that she gave to God, the more of God replaced her. He had saved her from her, and her old self was history. While being emptied of the devil's junk was a blessing, being filled with God Himself was and will always be the best thing that has ever happened to her. She could finally exhale and genuinely smile, for her tomorrow was guaranteed to be bright. She now has the desire to be consistent in her praise, in her walk, and in her relationship with Christ and others. She prays that others would not only be saved, but surrendered, so that they too can receive total deliverance for the glory of God.

*So if the Son sets you free, you will be free indeed.
— John 8:36 (NIV)*

As a child, she would look upon the walls of almost every house she entered and stare at man's depicted image of Jesus Christ. It seemed like the eyes on these pictures would follow her whenever and wherever she moved. She would move slowly while looking into his eyes, and sometimes quickly with jerking motions to trick him and shift his eyes. Similar to those man-made, fake images of Jesus Christ, the real Jesus Christ had been watching her and had been with her all along throughout her life; whenever and wherever she moved. Today, her eyes are finally fixed on Him as well; whenever and wherever He moves.

*My eyes are fixed on you, Sovereign Lord; in you I take refuge—do not give me over to death.*
*— Psalm 141:8 (NIV)*

Everything that she went through in life has prepared her for the present time. The many people that she comes in contact with on a daily basis at work and in her personal life are hurting, suicidal, addicted, mentally ill, physically pained, or spiritually entrapped. Yet, they are *still* God's children. It is only by the grace of God that she is able to "handle" difficult people with difficult circumstances. As a humble servant, she cannot allow herself to look down on them. She can only look directly at them, into the eyes of her old self with compassion and hope. If she could go from worshipping crack cocaine, the "rock" of hell, to worshipping Jesus Christ, The Rock of Heaven, she believed so could they.

*The LORD is my rock, my fortress and my deliverer; my God is my rock, in whom I take refuge, my shield and the horn of my salvation, my stronghold.*
*— Psalm 18:2 (NIV)*

When she finally got sick and tired enough of her life, she surrendered and gave her old life away to God, and became a daughter of the Most High King! Her old identity was self-centered and in direct conflict with her new identity in Jesus Christ. She is charged daily to put her old selfish characteristics to death and replace them with His. It is a miracle today that her record is clean. Yes, washed by the powerful blood of Jesus Christ!

*Throw off your old sinful nature and your former way of life, which is corrupted by lust and deception. Instead, let the Spirit renew your thought and attitudes. Put on your new nature, created to be like God – truly righteous and holy.*
*- Ephesians 4:22-24 (NLT)*

Some people have never spent a day behind bars, yet they are housed in a maximum-security facility known as "themselves". They have been sentenced to torment and destruction, and are blinded by darkness. Their vision is blurred to the truth and they squint in the presence of light. They are enslaved to selfishness and fleshly desires, and until they accept Christ and surrender all, they will never be paroled.

Yet and still, in receiving God's grace, there is hope for freedom and wholeness, with the promise of life and happiness even after.

*The thief comes only to steal and kill and destroy. I came that they may have life and have it abundantly.*
*– John 10:10 (ESV)*

# About the Author

**Andrea Grayson** is a small town country girl with big dreams. She earned her Associate's degree in Business Administration from Southeastern Oklahoma College, and today she works for the Oklahoma Department of Mental Health and Substance Abuse Services.

In her profession she is blessed daily with the opportunity to assist individuals like her former self. She one day aspires to own and manage a recovery and transitional home for underprivileged families in her hometown of Idabel, Oklahoma.

As she remains sober and continues in her walk with Christ, each day she must choose to do the next right thing.

She is the mother of three sons, 13 grandchildren, the spiritual parent of many, and the epitome of God's grace before your eyes.

Made in the USA
Middletown, DE
12 June 2016